The Small Handbook of Fallacies

A GUIDE TO EXPOSING NONSENSE IN EVERYDAY LIFE (2ND ED.)

BEN SEPHRAN

Contact the author:

Twitter: *@truthfulheretic*

FaceBook: *https://www.facebook.com/AuthorBenSephran*

Website: *http://trippleblue.wordpress.com/*

E-mail: *thetruthfulheretic@gmail.com*

Copyright © 2015 by Ben Sephran
All Rights Reserved.

ISBN-10: 1482657104
ISBN-13: 978-1482657104

Contents

Notes on Second Edition: 5

Introduction 7

Good vs. Bad argument 8

Logical Fallacies, Bad Arguments 9

    1.   Appeal to tradition..9

    2.   Appeal to Popular Idea (Ad Populum) 11

    3.   Appeal to Authority 13

    4.   Appeal to force/emotions............................14

    5.   Ad Hominem (Poisoning the well) 16

    6.   False Dilemma (False Dichotomy).................19

    7.   Equivocation 20

    8.   Appeal to consequences 22

    9.   Begging the question 23

    10.   Straw man fallacy.....................................24

    11.   Appeal to ignorance 27

    12.   "Post Hoc, Ergo Propter Hoc" 29

    13.   Unhealthy Example 31

    14.   Fallacy of Composition/Division.................33

    15.   Hasty Generalisation 35

    16.   Special Pleading 36

    17.   Red Herring 37

    18.   Fallacy of Fallacy 38

Notes..41

References: 43

Final word: How to deal with fallacies? 45

For further reading:...47

Intelligence: "Not because you think you know everything without questioning, but rather because you question everything you think you know."

- An internet meme

Notes on Second Edition:

I would like to thank friends and strangers who read the first edition and commented on it, particularly commenters on Amazon.com and Goodreads.

Some suggested that I add more examples and increase the quality of already existing ones. I did change some of the examples for this edition and I will keep working on bettering my work both in terms of quantity and quality (although I would like to keep the book relatively small to incorporate the title).

Others mentioned that my examples seem one sided. They look mostly anti-religious, and though they may be valid, they give an impression of one sidedness.

I firmly agree that illogical does not belong to a particular political party, left, right and centre, religious or nonreligious. Nor it is by any means correct to accuse members of different faiths of always being irrational. Illogical is an unfortunate condition of human species (including myself), and no one is infallible in that regard. If the purpose of this book is to engage as many young people as possible, then I also must consider incorporating more examples from all different beliefs.

That being said, I admit that my own experiences affect my choices for examples. And, that there are certain groups that (at least to my knowledge) have committed more fallacies than the others (Creationists for example). But hopefully as time passes by I will come across more examples from opposite sides of different political spectrums and beliefs.

At the end I would like to thank the readers for their constructive criticism and humbly ask for forgiveness for any of the possible mistakes I have made in advance.

Note: I had initially added a new section (Statistical Falsehoods) to the book. I have removed this section due to the fact that it was riddled with inaccuracies in terminology, and it also seemed out of place. I will work on what I had built in that section to correct it and expand it in both quality and quantity and make it (hopefully) into a new short book. I believe that subject is worth it.

Signed: Ben Sephran, October 2015.

Introduction

We are human beings. We used to be Homo erectus, we surpassed our other Homo cousins (such as Neanderthals), and now we are Homo sapiens. Without a doubt, we progressed. A painful, slow and most of the time dangerous progress, but progress nonetheless. And now that we are here, we may as well ask the question which perhaps enabled our ancestors to reach where they did: "Why?"

There are a combination of reasons for why we progress; why we, human beings, are beyond any other living creature on this planet. Even the smartest species of mammals, even the closest to us, our Chimpanzee cousins, have not been able to know more and be more than our children of a very young age.

We may have gained a lot of advantages in our path of evolution, but one advantage remains the reason why we evolve, even today. That is our language, our ability to make a claim, say what we think, and reason for its truth value. The way of the argument and reason. The ability to agree or disagree with each other, to ask "Why?" and to answer it. It may very well have all started with that first homo [1], around two million years ago, suddenly asking that very same powerful question: "Why?"

This handbook is mostly designed to be a simple guideline for those who wish to start learning more about logic. It could also be used as a small workshop for schools and teachers in order to get the next generation closer to a rational understanding of the world.

Good vs. Bad argument

A logical argument is not simply a discussion between two or more people, it is a set of statements together in a certain structure. It is the support of one statement (conclusion), based on some other statements (premises). A good argument is those set of premises which will necessarily result the conclusion, and has to meet certain criteria:

- Well-formed structure,
- Relevant premises,
- Reasonable, clear and sound premises,
- Internally consistent,

A fallacy on the other hand is an argument that does not meet the criteria above. Any problem with what came above will result in a faulty argument, and faulty arguments do not result in giving an acceptable conclusion. Keep in mind that this does not mean the conclusion is necessarily *wrong*, it means that the conclusion cannot be accepted in the light of the presented argument.

Before going ahead with introduction of the logical fallacies, it is worth mentioning the number zero fallacy, and that is making a claim without an argument to support it. We all at some point have heard the phrase "But that's just my opinion". An opinion is not an argument, and that statement is in fact *the* none-argument. It's a way of running away for those who wish never to give any reason for what they perceive to be true. Those who only wish to have conclusions, and only wish to stop any progress which could be achieved through conversation [2].

Logical Fallacies, Bad Arguments

What comes below is a rough list of the most common fallacies which we hear nowadays from homophobic groups, religious fanatics and fundamentalists, and of course politicians and many more [3]. Each fallacy is briefly defined and is accompanied with related examples. I have tried to find at least one example from the real world of news and politics for each section, since they are much more interesting that a made up example, and frankly quite easy to find.

1. Appeal to tradition

Trying to persuade other by an appeal to their feelings and respect for a certain tradition. In other words:

- X is traditional
- Therefore X is good (or acceptable)

The reason this line of argument is fallacious is a hidden premise: "Whatever is traditional is acceptable". Immediately we realize such is not the case. Slavery and sexism were (and still are) traditions in different societies. We now do not consider them acceptable, and if we find them in a society today (such as Islamic societies) we condemn them. *Tradition is not reason.*

Example: During the course of her carrier, the prime minister of Australia, Julia Gillard, was questioned about the issue of gay marriage numerous times. Her replies were usually a matter of dancing around the question, starting with "Our position…" or "I and the Labour party have a clear position…" She usually avoided answering "Why?", instead repeated her disagreement in different ways.

However, there were some cases in which she did try to answer, and that is when our first fallacy is clearly shown. As the Daily Telegraph report from 2011 reads, Ms. Gillard tried to justify her disagreement with gay marriage as follows (Unknown, 2011a):

> "I think that there are some important things from our past that need to continue to be part of our present and part of our future," she said. "If I was in a different walk of life, if I'd continued in the law and was partner of a law firm now, I would express the same view, that I think for our culture, for our heritage, the Marriage Act and marriage being between a man and a woman has a special status."

Surely, if we wish to agree with Ms. Gillard, as we saw above we may as well continue slavery and misogyny. After all, they were important parts of our culture and heritage. There is one more thing that is indeed not traditional: Women as prime ministers. I suspect Ms. Gillard should have resigned according to her own logic.

This fallacy is also important to note in defence of things that may actually be good. Take the whole different celebrations (such as Christmas) that most cultures have around the world. If one asks what is the point of celebrating Christmas (or any other celebration), one may wish to defend the so called *tradition* of Christmas simply because it is a part of many cultures or heritage. But such defence falls into the same category of fallacious argument: If Christmas (or any celebration) is *good*, that does not come from it being a tradition. Traditions are not reasons.

In such case we may wish to argue about the good effects that such celebrations can have on the society. Or perhaps based on the fact that having such celebrations can have positive impact on individual lives.

2. Appeal to Popular Idea (Ad Populum)

The notion that an idea is true solely because it is a popular idea or accepted by a large number of people.

In some aspects this fallacy is similar to appeal to tradition, because many traditions are also popular amongst a specific group of people or a nationality. However popular ideas themselves are not always traditions.

Example: A very simple example of this fallacy came when I had an argument with a housemate:

> **Housemate**: *I don't clean the house because no one else does!*

> **Me**: *Not true, but even if it was, so what? The fact that others don't do their duty doesn't reduce your duty.*

The fact that "No one else does it!" Or, that "Everyone else is doing it!" does not make a statement right or wrong. This can be as boring as the matter of tedious house chores, or as serious as the injury or death of people. *Mass hysteria* is the same type of thinking; that something is happening or is true because everyone else seems to think so.

There are many instances of mass hysteria that we can point to. One of the most famous is the 1938 radio adaptation of H. G. Wells' novel "The War of the Worlds" by Orson Welles. The program was so similar to real news that many people took it seriously.

Another more recent (and more hilarious if I may say) example of a belief because of mass hysteria is known as "The Hindu milk miracle" (Higgins, 2008). In 1995, it was reported that a statue of Lord Ganesha (a Hindu god) was "drinking a spoonful of milk". This caused thousands of Hindus to rush towards temples all over the world and begin to feed the status! They all believed that these statues were actually drinking the milk simply because everyone else seemed to see it happen.

Even after scientists explained that the reason for this was physical and the milk was in fact running down the body of the statue as a result of the capillary action combined with gravity, many believers still thought that this was a miracle. Later it was claimed that the statues had "stopped drinking milk". As if they had ever begun to do so! They all believed each other's words instead of even believing their own eyes.

Let us end with a humorous story about this fallacy:

Mr. John Smith was always bothered by the sound of children playing in the street right below his window. On a particularly hot day in June, he just had enough. He opened his window and shouted "Santa has come early this year and is giving up free candy just down the block!" The kids started running down the street to collect the candy from Santa.

Suddenly Mr. Smith jumped into action, running towards the door without wearing his shoes. Mrs. Smith asked him "What the hell are you doing John?" to which he responded "If there really was no candy, they wouldn't have been running so fast to get it. I'm afraid I won't be in time to get any!"

3. Appeal to Authority

The fallacy that the notion X is true, only because authority Y says so.

No matter who the authority is, God, Prophet, holy book, the President, Mr. John Smith, or even one's self; the authority still needs a reason to believe a certain notion, and that reason has to be clear. Sometimes, the reason is perfectly clear. A doctor has a specialty and a definite insight into the illnesses he or she has specialized in. It is perfectly reasonable to assume a specialist has good reasons for her claims. Therefore it won't be fallacious to back a claim about one's health and cite the doctor as the source of it.

To make this clearer, we could put it this way: Authority cannot be replaced as a premise of an argument, or as the reason behind a claim. However, a legitimate authority can be put as the source for reasons behind a claim.

Example: There is quite an interesting issues on morality which could be pointed out under this fallacy. A lot of moral claims given by fundamentalists turn out to be purely fallacious, on both fronts: replacing the authority with reason, or appealing to an authority which by no means is even remotely close to being a specialist on the subject of moral claims. Sometimes it is even worse, the authority turns out to be completely devoid of any sense of morality.

One of these particular issues is the law itself, when the law is presented as the only reason for the correctness of a notion. In a back and forth conversation with some pro-guns after the shooting in Sandy Hook elementary school (in 2012), they kept pointing out that "We have the right to have guns, our constitution is clear about it." and I kept asking them "It's true that the law in US allows people to have weapons, but why do you think it's the right thing to do? Why the law is right? What is the reason?"

The law does not make a notion automatically right simply because it is *the law*. There are reasons behind what our politicians decide to legislate, and simply pointing at a certain law does not make a claim right.

Perhaps the worst of all appeals to authority are the claims from religious fundamentalists on the subject of moral values. In arguments with religious fanatics, "X is wrong" is a notion that is usually backed up by "Because God has commanded it". Obviously God (any God) is by no means a legitimate authority on moral subjects. Most of it could be because God never seems to clearly answer questions about his reasons for a particular commandment. And moreover, by reading most religious books, we immediately realize most Gods are worse than psychopaths. How could they ever be legitimate authorities on moral subjects [4]?

4. Appeal to force/emotions

Trying to persuade others by means of coercion or by appealing to their emotions. This is a more obvious form of appealing to consequences.

Example: There may be a lot of cases in which this fallacy happens in our ordinary lives. I remember my own dad's responses to my question of "Why?" Which were usually given as a shout of "Because I say so, and you know what happens when you don't listen to me boy!" It was obvious to me, even at my very young age, that his way of coercion does not make things he wanted right. There must have been reasons behind them other than his sheer force.

Perhaps the simplest and most common examples are some students at the end of the semester "You cannot fail me Professor Smith, if that happens I'll be expelled/ my dad will kill me."

Professor Smith may be quite sorry that these things may happen, he may even consider passing the student, but there is no logical reason for that. The argument is flawed since it only appeals to emotions and abandons the reason behind a fail grade, that the student simply does not know enough about the subject at hand.

Sometimes however, fallacies in general and appeal to emotions in particular create funny scenarios. I came across the following humorous story some years ago, which is based on this fallacy: There was a very poor writer who lived in a very bad state. He wrote a book and took it to a publisher as a last-ditch effort to earn some money. The publisher asked: "What's the book about?" to which the writer responded: "It's a story about a woman who's in love with a young man. They marry each other, and she gets pregnant, but the man is eaten by a shark, the child is born dead, and she finally commits suicide from heart-break. Also, if you don't publish the story, its writer will die of hunger!"

Sadly, it is not always fun and games. Propaganda is another less common form of this fallacy [5]. It is a media based movement devoid of any substantial reason, but based on excitation of the feelings that people may have on a particular subject. An example for movement is the so called "pro-life" movement in US. Most of what is presented by the pro-life could be considered as propaganda. Read a part of the poem written from an unborn child's mouth against abortion (Hauck, 2009):

> *please don't let them kill me,*
> *it wasn't my fault mommy.*
> *and if you think you're doing what's right*
> *then ask yourself, what if it was me?*

Surely there is nothing fallacious in poetry as an art, but the fallacy happens if a person only relies on these emotional means rather than trying to argue logically for a position. Remember that no argument is presented, if one tries to argue against abortion, one has to do so by means of reason and evidence, not just by writing poems of this sort, designed only to provoke emotional response instead of giving a message by means of reasoning. Most propaganda exists exactly because there are no good reasons to appeal to, only emotions.

5. Ad Hominem (Poisoning the well)

Ad Hominem simply means personal attack. It is the argument that someone is wrong because there is something wrong with him or her. This fallacy is essentially <u>the fallacy of attacking the arguer instead of the argument.</u>

Example: This is a paragraph of a blog post by a user named "The answer girl". She obviously is far from having any acceptable answers, because of the following post, which is about the rejection of homosexuality being natural (Unknown, 2011b):

"But the proof offered, my dear friends, needs to be towards the unbiased side of the spectrum. This means that those pro-homosexuality and/or LGBT supporting websites shouldn't be part of your argument, since – in most cases – the information is biased and misleading. A friend of mine told me she was reading a book on this type of research, for example, and the authors were a homosexual couples. One would assume that information might have been mishandled or the research conducted might have been leading (i.e. forced), for example."

One must be very careful regarding the notion of *bias*. In research method and statistics there is indeed a serious case for being biased, but the nature of the research itself is very determining in such cases. As you can see above, our answer girl is not trying to go after any evidence to suggest the results of research done by LGBT supporting websites or books are indeed biased, she is doing the very basic case of Ad Hominem attack: She claims off the bat, without reading any such research, that the information is biased because it is given by LGBT supporters.

It does not matter who gives the information, a Nazi may claim racism true, but he or she is not wrong *because* he is a Nazi. If we wish to prove anyone wrong, we need to prove their claims or arguments wrong.

This fallacy could be very tricky at times. In a lot of TV shows we can more or less hear things like "You are a member of X, obviously you agree with anything that your associated group says!" But a person's political party, race or the religion they belong to is irrelevant to the truth value of the claims they make, or the structure of their arguments. The following section from the interview between Josh Zepp (Huff Post Live) and Suey Park (as Feminist guest) perfectly demonstrates this. Park at the time had created the #CancelColbert on twitter over satirical tweets that comedian Stephen Colbert had made:

> *Zepp*: *"To get upset about the use of the word orientalism in a satirical context strikes me as misguided."*

> *Park*: *"It is incredibly patronising for you to paint these questions this way. Especially as a white man. I don't expect you to understand what people of colour are actually saying with regards to #cancelcolbert."*

> *Zepp*: *"Being a white man doesn't prevent me from being able to think and doesn't prevent me from having thought, reason, perspective on things. I didn't give up my ability to have an intellectual conversation when I was born."*

> *Park*: *"I know but while white men think they are entitles to talk over me, they definitely think they are entitles to minimalize my experiences. And they definitely think they are so exempt and so logical compared to women who are painted as emotional right?"*

> *Zepp*: *"No, No one is minimalizing your experiences and no one is minimalizing your right to have an opinion. It's just a stupid opinion."*

> *Park*: *"You just called my opinion stupid [..] and I don't think I am going to enact the labour to explain why that's incredibly offensive and patronizing."*

Zepp couldn't have said it better. It seems that Ms. Park forgot the simple fact that the colour of one's skin does not determine one's capability to understand things. Nor does one's gender. When she could not defend her position logically, she simply shifted to attack the person who was criticizing her.

6. False Dilemma (False Dichotomy)

Trying to persuade others by presenting false alternatives as a solution to a problem, then asserting that one of those has to be the right answer.

Example: Sometimes the examples regarding this fallacy are humorously simplistic. For instance let me prove to you that you have eaten my sandwich: "It was either you who ate my sandwich, or a pink unicorn. Since it was not a pink unicorn, because obviously they do not exist, therefore it must have been you!"

However there are other instances in which this fallacy becomes serious, very serious. This again could happen in our ordinary lives or within social or political movements. Just consider the statement "If you're not with us, then you're against us". A lot of people may not agree with something, but this does not put them in the same category. This is usually a fascistic statement: Whoever does not agree with me is my enemy.

Another very good example of this is most of creationists' arguments [6]. Almost all keep trying to reject evolution, as if rejecting evolution will automatically prove creationism to be true.

1. *It is either created by [my] God or evolved through the process of natural selection,*

2. *It is not evolved through the process of natural selection,*

C => *It is created by [my] God.*

The way to tackle this argument is almost as interesting: We may simply add one or more horns to the dilemma. Therefore, for the above example we may casually ask: "How about Lamarckism then? If evolution has not happened, maybe Lamarck was right? Maybe Ancient Egyptians were right, and it was actually Amon-Ra who according to Egyptian mythology spoke the name of different things and they jumped into existence. Maybe Scientologists are right, maybe Buddhists or any other myth about how living creatures and human beings came to be."

7. Equivocation

Using word(s) that have two or more different meanings (e.g. gambling, faith, etc.) in an argument, in a way that appears to have the same meaning. This is usually used as a way to confuse others.

Example: In a YouTube video of the former Republican presidential candidate "Michele Bachmann" (Unknown, 2011c), a schoolgirl asks her about what the government should do to support LGBT community. Avoiding the original question and jumping to gay marriage, Bachman answered: "We all have the same civil right, and there should be no special rights for anyone."

Meaning that gay marriage is a "special right" to be given to the gay community. Of course, she equivocated between civil rights (law), whatever has already been legislated, and equal rights, which are exactly what requested by the LGBT community based on unfairness of the opportunity provided for straight couples by legally recognizing them as married, but not for gay relationships.

Another good example is as the argument sometimes made by religious speakers. Consider the following fictional (but certainly similar to a lot of what we hear from preachers) quote from a fanatical preacher about Atheism: "Religion is one of the most important things in a person's life. And I ask you, what is very important for Atheists? What do they happily do when asked about their convictions? They deny the existence of God! In fact this is so important for them that they waste no time rejecting his existence and argue endlessly about how the faithful are wrong. What could be more religious than that? Is this *religion* not what they condemn? Are they not hypocrites?"

The equivocation is clear since we immediately realize that *religion* is not the same as *religion*. If my partner tells me that "Football is your religion" surely he means it is very important for me. But what he does not mean is that "Football is a set of divinely inspired beliefs and values which is institutionalized by a specific hierarchy."

Fortunately our vocabulary is not filled with words that could always be used in the same argument with different meanings. However, this fallacy could potentially be very sneaky, since we may not see it clearly in a verbal debate or argument. Therefore studying and reading could enable us discover this type of fallacy very efficiently.

21

8. Appeal to consequences

It is the rejection/acceptance of a conclusion based on the undesirability/desirability of the consequences of that notion, regardless of the reasoning behind it.

Example: The infamous YouTube sensation *Bananaman* (his actual name is Ray Comfort), published a version of Darwin's *The Origin of Species* with his own so called "Introduction". The following quote is taken from there (Comfort, 2009):

> *"In promoting the idea that humans were merely animals and accidents of nature, the natural consequence of Darwinism was to overturn the traditional Judeo-Christian values on the sacredness of human life. The legacy of Darwin's theory can be seen in the rise of eugenics, euthanasia, racism, infanticide, and abortion."*

That quote is a part of an entire section named "The Hit List", full of the same basic fallacy of appealing to consequences. *If* we apply Darwin's theory to this, *if* we apply it to that, this and that unpleasant consequences happen. He mentions Hitler and Nazism, completely disregards the roots of Hitler's views, and blames it only on the consequences of believing Darwinian evolution.

Obviously, Darwin's theory is a scientific theory based on evidence from the natural world, and the undesired consequences of applying it to society or racism [7] have clearly no weight in disproving it.

Sometimes the examples are not as obvious, and not fallacious: Consider the whole debate about tax policies (not just in US, this happens all over the world), these debates are

22

usually about the consequences of preferring one policy over another, but we do not tend to regard them as bad arguments. In fact, quite the reverse. The reason is simply the fact that the argument itself is *for* the consequences, and one premise of the argument in favour of tax policy X is always "Tax policy X creates desirable result for the society".

9. Begging the question

This is simply circular logic, and it means the premises have the conclusion or a part of it in them.

Example: This fallacy is an important one, and happens in a lot of arguments we stumble upon, from simple everyday life situations to sophisticated philosophical statements. Running in circles is sometimes a humorous and pointless activity, something that we all may have done in the past.

A: Santa only gives presents to nice children.

B: But Why?

A: If he didn't, no nice child would get any presents for Christmas.

As we see there is no new message in what came above. Santa gives presents to nice children, because nice children receive presents from Santa. Now, this could happen in a little more serious way as well. For example when a holy book is used to prove a God exists, and the same God is used to give credibility to the same book:

The Bible is a miracle from God, and we all know that miracles are signs from God that prove beyond doubt he exists.

23

Miracles prove the existence of God. But why are miracles credible? Because God sends them to us. Again no new message is given, and the argument fails to give us credible information about miracles or the existence of God. As you may guess, no fallacy belongs to a specific religion or culture, for an example of the same sort from the world of Islam, let's see an ontological argument for the existence of god which goes as follows (short form of Mulla-Sadra's argument):

1. *Whatever existence that has all the perfections is called God,*
2. *All other forms of existence have to come from the perfect existence,*
3. *There are other forms of existence,*
C => God exists.

The existence of God is assumed in the premises, while it needs to be proved in conclusion. In other words, there should *be* a God (i.e. the perfect existence) to have the property of perfection.

There is another very famous philosophical statement, the most famous amongst not just philosophers but people as well, and that is "I think therefore I am". According to what we read about begging the question fallacy, we immediately realize that Descartes assumes he exists in the "I think". But this is the very same thing that he wants to prove in "Therefore I am". This is indeed a case of begging the question [8].

10. Straw man fallacy

As the name suggests, this is an attack on a straw man: When someone pretends to criticise one thing, but in fact is criticising something else that him/herself has put on its place.

Example: A conversation between two friends is not unlikely to go as follows,

> *A: Money is not everything.*

> *B: If money was nothing, you would not have worked your entire life just to make more of it.*

> *A: But I did not say money was nothing, I simply said it was not everything.*

As it is obvious from A's response to B, during the course of conversation B changes A's original claim about money ("Money is not everything" into "Money is nothing"), and then attacks the second statement as if it was A's claim to begin with.

Straw man fallacy is quite common in our everyday lives. Imagine a conversation between two people about the use of marijuana:

> *A: We should allow medical use of marijuana because scientists have shown its use can help some patients with their treatment.*

> *B: If we were to let everyone have access to all drugs because it can make some ill people feel better, then the whole society will become addicted. People will start using these drugs left and right!*

> *A: I didn't say that! I just said we should let some patients have access to marijuana!*

B: Are you calling me an idiot? How dare you!

Of course, this is childishly simplistic. But this easily happens when someone twists other people's words. Now, when the same type of fallacy shows itself in sophisticated political or social discussions, it may become harder to detect. Consider this hypothetical (but not unlikely to happen) conversation in a TV show regarding economic systems:

> **Host:** *I believe we need to bring more equality and social justice to our laws regarding the bottom quintile of the income distribution in our society.*
>
> **Guest:** *But Socialism failed miserably in the Soviet Union, and the situation was horrible for everyone, including the bottom quintile.*
>
> **Host:** *That's a Straw man. I did not say we need to become Socialist. I was saying we have a huge gap in our income distribution, and we need to bring in closer to equality, not to make it equal like a socialist would suggest.*

As we see the guest is creating a false dilemma as well, by pretending there could only be two possible choices of economic systems (Capitalism vs. Socialism), and then the straw man plays in by asserting that the host means Socialism.

There are two things to note here: One is, since this fallacy is very common, it is easy to get paranoid about it. We should be vigilant about the *misrepresentation* of our arguments, but we should not expect others to always directly quote us. Any small change in what we said is not necessarily a misrepresentation.

26

Secondly, we should not confuse this fallacy with others such as *appeal to consequences*.

11. Appeal to ignorance

This fallacy is also sometimes called "Shifting the burden of proof", and it is simply put the fallacious argument that "You cannot prove me wrong, therefore I have to be right".

Example: A conversation that happened between me and one of my uncles went as follows,

> *A: There are mysterious forces in the universe, and some people can use those forces.*
>
> *B: But how do you know?*
>
> *A: Some years ago I travelled to India, and saw an Indian guru who could float in the air.*
>
> *B: How do you know that he had unknown powers?*
>
> *A: Because no scientist was able to explain how he could float in the air. So there should be a force he is using which is out of scientist's reach.*
>
> *B: Magicians do things that the best physicists cannot explain. But nobody suggests they are tapping into mysterious powers.*

Just the fact that scientists (or anyone else for that matter) cannot explain a phenomenon does not stand for the existence of "Mysterious forces". If one wants to put forward and defend such a notion, one must give evidence for the notion itself. "Scientists don't know" can only prove that scientists don't know, and by no means gives a claim of that sort any credibility.

There is a peculiar tendency within human species to attribute reasons to what we do not understand. Superstition by default falls under the category of this fallacy: In the past there was much we could not explain, therefore we made stories about our ignorance, simply because we did not understand. Ironically, even in the modern world in which we know much more than we use to, some of us still cling to this fallacy. *God of the gaps* is the best example here.

A: Do scientists know what happened before big bang?

B: I don't think they have discovered that yet, how come?

A: But there must have been a cause for big bang, and this cause has to be God.

B: Just the fact that we don't know what happened before the big bang does not mean "God did it". That claim needs to be judged on its own merits.

Another very good example of such fallacy happened in an internet discussion with an Islamist about truth value of Islamic claims, as he told the following story: "A terrorist attack on an Islamic settlement caused the death of numerous people, of whom one Ayat-O-Allah [9] was the most pious. Since the attack was by an explosion, his body was blown to pieces, and not all were found. One night after the incident, his wife dreamed about him, and in her dream she saw his body trapped in a wall. When she woke up and told of her dream, other found some of the pieces in a wall near the explosion."

He then concluded that "This must be the power of Allah" from the "unseen universe" (A concept in the Quran is to have faith in the unseen [Quran: Albagharah: verse 2]). Simply the fact that we may not be able to explain such an event [10] does not give any credibility to the concept of the "Unseen universe" or "Allah did it".

Any claim needs to be justified based on the evidence in favour or against it, and not knowing something does not provide any evidence for any claim. Not knowing is simply not knowing, nothing more.

12. "Post Hoc, Ergo Propter Hoc"

In Latin, the phrase above means "After this, therefore because of this". It stands for the fallacy that since something happened after another, it must have been caused by it.

Example: This is the favourite fallacy of the so called *mediums* or *psychics*. Imagine Mr. John Smith who has lost his wedding ring goes to famous psychic Ms. Jane Fortune in order for her to find his ring for him [11]. Of course Ms. Fortune surely can find the ring, the only matter is the ghosts she is talking to require a fee, and obviously Mr. Smith pays the required price. Say, if Mr. Smith finds the ring the next morning in the liner of his coat, does this mean that him paying Ms. Fortune *caused* the discovery of the ring? Was it not so that it happened exactly after that?

This fallacy happens in another instance which is very similar to the above case. The so called *faith healers*. This subject of being healed with faith came up in a discussion with a Muslim correspondent in a public forum about the power of God. The story he told is a common theme with all these so called *faith healing* stories: "There was a very pious Shia Ayat-O-Allah named Boroojerdi. At the time that he was still studying, he needed to wear glasses and he had an excruciating pain in his eyes. One day during the yearly Shia mourning ceremony of Hussein, he thought to rub some dirt falling from the mourners bodies on his eyes as a sign of his devotion, and prayed to Allah for his problem. And *immediately* after that he got healed and never had any problems with his eyes ever again. What could possibly be the reason for this except the power of God?"

Bizarre stories to any sane mind. But aside from the truth value of the claims made, assuming this is all true, the story itself falls prey to the same fallacy. The question "How do you know it was Allah?" cannot be properly answered. Simply because something happened after another does not mean it was caused by that, and here simply because the person in question asked the invisible none-comprehensible Allah for help and was *healed* does not mean it was that God who did it.

This fallacy is not just about invisible forces. Sometimes however complex things are over simplified with much simpler explanations, and this is one of the instances this fallacy could sneak in. Consider the following conversation as an example:

> **A:** *I think Christianity is a great system of governance.*
>
> **B:** *How come?*
>
> **A:** *Just look at the Emperor Constantine and the fact that right after he converted to Christianity, he was able to defeat his enemies and unite the Roman Empire.*

> **B:** *Just because he was able to do all those things after turning to Christianity does not mean Christianity is the reason behind that. Maybe he himself was a great ruler or commander. Maybe he was just lucky.*

And yet again, we see that same fallacy, but this time as an oversimplification.

13. Unhealthy Example

Claiming a general rule about a specific subject based on another seemingly similar matter, usually given as an example.

Example: This is not a very common fallacy, but quite amusing to see it at work. Sometimes, when we want to be sentimental or try to explain things for others in an easy way, this fallacy could creep in.

There was a story going around via e-mail about a conversation between a professor and his students on the subject of God. This still could be found on the internet, and the following is my reconstruction of that conversation:

> **P:** *If God is omnipotent, omniscient and omnibenevolent, then there shouldn't be any bad things in the world. But we can see evil all over, just watching the news for fifteen minutes is enough. Therefore there cannot be such a God.*
>
> **S:** *Sir, may I ask a question?*
>
> **P:** *Of course.*
>
> **S:** *Does cold exist?*
>
> **P:** *Of course it exists. Have you ever gone out in the winter?*

S: No sir, there is no such thing as cold. Cold is only the absence of heat in form of energy. Now, does darkness exist?

P: Of course it does.

S: No, darkness is only the absence of light. Now sir I ask, does evil exist?

P: Yes it does.

S: No sir, evil does not exist. It is only the absence of good that we call evil.

There is something fundamentally wrong with what the student concludes after the discussion. Again, going back to the theme of asking "Why?", we can immediately see that no reason is given to "Why evil does not exist?". The only things we can see are examples that the student gives, and though they seem similar, do not answer the question "Why?". Even their similarity is only linguistic, and irrelevant: Both examples are of the physical world, but *good* and *evil* are not.

The most notable problem with this fallacy is that no argument is presented to support the conclusion.

Another intriguing example of this is a follow up on the ontological argument which we discussed on the "begging the question" fallacy, and it goes as follows:

Existence is like the light. As the light come from an ultimate source that is radiant on its own, independent of all others, existence also needs an ultimate source. That source again has to be independent and higher than all other forms of existence, because all others come from it. We all know what we call this ultimate existence God.

Again by asking the question "Why does existence need to have come from an ultimate existence?" we realize that the argument above does not answer this, instead tries to justify its claim based on comparing it with the light.

We could approach this fallacy by an intriguing method. For instance pointing out to the aspects of the similar case put forward which are not very plausible for the arguer's conclusion. For the case above for instance we could point out maybe God is also an object without any will, just like the sources of light are.

We also need to keep in mind that examples are not fallacies, they are usually quite useful. Of course given that an argument is indeed presented and the examples are simply follow ups on the argument and for better understanding of one's position.

14. Fallacy of Composition/Division

The fallacy of composition could be describes as "What is true about each member of a group is also true about the group itself". The fallacy of division is quite the reverse; it is "What is true about a specific group is also true about each member of that group".

Example: This type of fallacy is important for many arguments, from the most abstract to the most practical. Consider the following argument about how we should invest in economic activities:

> *I think a reason for these recurring recessions is because we are not careful with our money as individuals. If everybody invests safely in short term activities that can easily be*

cashed, then the society could be much safer in terms of economic investment.

An economist would immediately point out that such claim as quite absurd. The problem is, since *everybody* invests in short term activities, with the first sign of economic downturn, *everybody* will try to cash in their short term investments. And that is exactly why *everybody* will be far worse, and most definitely less safe. Best case scenario would actually be a combination of both short and long-term investments, so that if we fail in one, we may have some compensation in the other.

Another good example of this fallacy is what we can see in the so called "cosmological arguments", one form of the arguments for the existence of God(s). What follows is generally how the argument proceeds:

1. *Every effect has a cause,*
2. *The universe is an effect,*
C => *The universe has a cause*

Looking at the premises of the argument, we can clearly see that it is trivially true. But trivially true about the things *in* the universe. Surely, it does not follow that a statement that is true *in* the universe is also true *about* the universe. In other words, the first premise is true about every member of the universe, but not necessarily true about the universe itself.

On the other hand, the fallacy of composition tends to be a little more obvious. For instance, a cat maybe very cute, but it may have the ugliest tale in the world! Or, Imagine John, a young car-lover who has just bought the latest model of

Porsche. To John's surprise, the car breaks down after only 200 miles. When the mechanic suggests that there is a problem with the engine, John claims "But this is the best car in the world, how could there be anything wrong with its engine?". Of course, we clearly see that the car maybe the best in the world, but its engine may not. The engine is only a part of the car, and whatever may be true about the car may not be true about the engine.

15. Hasty Generalisation

The fallacy that if something is true about a small fraction of a group, which does not accurately represent it, it has to be true about the entire group as well.

Example: The most trivial examples of this fallacy could easily happen in our everyday conversation. For example, say that Mary and John go to Scotland, and they are taking a train to Edinburgh. Along the way, they happen to pass a farm and can see a black cow grazing in the field. If Mary turns to John and says: "Look! Cows in Scotland are black!"; she has fallen into the hasty generalization fallacy.

This fallacy happens a lot in social matters, particularly in the age of media, and an attribute of some members of a particular faith or race is generalized to the whole group. Consider the following discussion between two friends after the events on 11th September:

> *A: From what happened on the day of the attack on twin towers we can clearly see the true nature of Muslims. They have no respect for other human beings and even their own lives.*

35

B: *From what happened we can only judge some fundamentalist Muslims, but surely not all Muslims are like that.*

This is not to say we cannot criticize members of different belief systems or the belief system itself, but if we wish to do so, we may not try to use these type of generalizations. Instead, we can use arguments based on accepted ideas within that belief system.

This fallacy could sometimes sneak in without the generalization being obvious. Imagine if we see in the news that there is a chicken in a farm, this time say in Yugoslavia, which can actually fly. Could we claim that "This shows some chickens can fly"? Surely not. That flying chicken is a special case, and cannot still be generalized to even to a subgroup of chickens (i.e. "some" chickens).

16. Special Pleading

Excluding situations, objects or people from principles or rules which usually should be applied to them, without providing a good reason.

Example: This is an interesting fallacy, because it plays an important role in usual conversations as well as having philosophical implication (particularly for philosophy of science). Take for example the case of two students, say, John and Jane, in a classroom. They both act disrespectfully towards the teacher, but when John is asked to describe both their behaviours, his answer is "I was not being disrespectful; I was just confidently challenging the teacher. It was Jane who was arrogant and impolite."

This fallacy plays an important role in philosophy of science. Scientific theories are laws and rules that we believe describe how the world works. Most philosophers of science agree that there should be no "special pleading" for a fact that seems to falsify a specific theory.

A famous example is Newton's worldview of physics, or *Newtonian paradigm*. It seemed for years that Mercury did not behave as the Newtonian worldview expected it to. Since *no special pleading* applied here, scientists (including Einstein) came up with other different theories that seemed to better describe reality, and in the end Einstein's theory of relativity finally succeeded in adequately explaining this phenomenon (Chalmers, 2011, p.140). If *special pleading* was to be allowed, then any theory could easily explain away things that seemed to falsify it, and no progress would have been achieved.

17. Red Herring

Red Herring is simply the fallacy of diversion. Instead of addressing the argument presented, the fallacy tries to divert the attention to other matters.

Example: One obvious example could be as follows,

> *A: I believe gay marriage should be legal, because it is only fair that homosexuals have the same opportunities as straight people do.*

> *B: But there are far more important things happening in the world. Think about how we are wasting time on these issues while people are dying of AIDS in Africa.*

A: What has that got to do with this? Of course that's important and we should talk about it, but it is irrelevant to the subject of gay marriage.

Of course there are a lot of important subject that require attention. But the existence of one does not diminish the importance of another. Sometimes this fallacy could be very hard to detect, or to deal with. For example consider the whole debate about torture:

"Liberals keep saying that torture is wrong because every human being has the right not to be tortured. But is it not more essential that every human being has the right to live? What if torturing someone can save lives through providing critical information of terrorist activities?"

The arguer does not address the main argument of those who disagree with him, instead he makes his own claims about torture. He may or may not be right in his own argument, but that is irrelevant to the other position. He first should address why the so called Liberals are wrong to suggest "every human being has the right not to be tortured".

18. Fallacy of Fallacy

Arguing that conclusion of an argument is false, because the argument is fallacious or wrong.

Example: This is a fitting fallacy to end this section of the book with, since it happens in form of a counter argument: "I don't find your argument logically sound, therefore your conclusion must be false."

Consider the following simple, but false argument:

1. *All mammals are made of living cells.*
2. *Sharks are mammals.*

C => Sharks are made of living cells.

This argument is clearly absurd, we obviously know sharks are not mammals. But the conclusion is in fact true: Sharks are indeed made of cells.

Example: Imagine the following discussion:

> *A: There is a monster in the Loch Ness! If there was not, so many people wouldn't have reported on it and wouldn't have believed in it.*

> *B: You are just appealing to the popular idea. The fact that many people believe in something doesn't make it true. All these fallacious arguments can only mean that there is no monster!*

Our good sceptic B in here unfortunately has fallen into the fallacy of fallacy argument. The fact that A's argument was fallacious does not make the conclusion of his argument necessarily false.

During this book we used many examples of fallacious theistic arguments in favour of the existence of a God. But with this fallacy it must be clear that we cannot argue "Your argument for the existence of your God is fallacious, therefore your God just can't exist."

There is no reason to believe the conclusion of an argument is necessarily false because the argument is faulty or has wrong premises. The only thing we can do is to say "Your argument does not achieve the goal of proving its conclusion". If a nonbeliever wishes to prove "There can be no God", s/he has to make an argument of their own.

It may look as if in this part we are undoing what we weaved during the whole book. But this simply is not the case. In many of the cases we can argue very well against the conclusions of bad arguments with our own good arguments. For example, in case of the Loch Ness monster sceptic B, s/he can simply argue: "If there was a true monster in Loch Ness, then we must have found a sign of it by now. It is a monster after all! Since we have not found any credible sign of such monster except word of mouth from people and blurry images, we can conclude that the existence of such monster is very unlikely, if not just built up stories."

Notes

[1] Literally!

[2] *Those people* usually tend to be religious fundamentalists or politicians. Of course it could indicate a comfortable delusion or utter dishonesty respectively.

[3] Of course, politicians are a perfect source for fallacies. Their dishonesty is astonishing, their ability to deceive almost unmatched by any other profession.

[4] Compare this with the case of legitimate authority who specializes on a subject; for example a scientist on his or her specialty. A legitimate authority is always prepared to provide reasons for what he or she believes.

[5] Any social movement based on propaganda is very dangerous exactly because of this. It plays with the crowds emotions, and the response is also often emotional and unpredictable.

[6] Creationists are a special bunch. One of the best learning activities in introductory logic and fallacies is reading their websites.

[7] One cannot apply evolution as a scientific theory to social or political parties without the role of an underlying ideology. In case of Hitler and Nazism the roots of the problem goes back as far as Hegel.

[8] Most philosophers agree that this is the case, including Descartes himself. But he never meant to give an actual *proof* for the existence of *I*. What he meant to point out was the

simple and trivially obvious fact that it is almost impossible to assume "I do not exist".

[9] An Ayat-O-Allah literally means "A sign from Allah" and is a title for a high ranking Shia religious leader.

[10] We actually do know a great deal about this, even if the story is true.

[11] Perhaps from the unseen universe?!

References:

Chalmers, A. F. 2011. What *is this Thing Called Science?*. 3rd ed. Open University Press. UK.

Darwin, C. (Author), R. Comfort (Introduction). 2009. *The Origin of Species: 150th Anniversary Edition.* Bridge-Logos Foundation. USA.

Dimitrova, Anelia. K. 2011. "Student challenges Bachmann on marriage". *YouTube* video. Accessed online, October 2015. http://www.youtube.com/watch?v=RenwNhL1Te0

Hauck, K. 2009. *helpless child (against abortion).* Accessed online, October 2015. http://www.poemhunter.com/poem/helpless-child-against-abortion/

Higgins, C. 2008. "The Hindu Milk Miracle". *Mental_floss.* Accessed online, November 2015. http://mentalfloss.com/article/18216/hindu-milk-miracle

Minespatch the channel. 2014. "Josh Zepp interviews Suey Park". *YouTube* video. Accessed online, October 2015. https://www.youtube.com/watch?v=MNK-e6nnFGY

Unknown. 2011a. "Australian PM Julia Gillard: Gay marriage against my upbringing". *The Daily Telegraph*. Accessed online, October 2015. http://www.dailytelegraph.com.au/news/pm-julia-gillard-gay-marriage-against-my-upbringing/story-e6freuy9-1226025009815

Unknown. 2011b. Thought on Homosexuality. *The Answer Girl (Tumblr Weblog).* Accessed online, October

2015. http://theanswergirl.tumblr.com/post/8790361207/thoughts-on-homosexuality

Final word: How to deal with fallacies?

Reading about fallacies and knowing them is important, not just because of us wanting to know about others' mistakes, but because of ourselves as well. If we know how to conduct an argument properly, or rather how not to conduct it improperly, we can proceed with more confidence in rational aspects of our lives, from everyday conversations to academic papers. It could also help us recognize fanatics, fundamentalists and charlatans much easier, seeing right through their claims of propaganda, lies or the false statistics they might throw around.

But even more important is to know how we can deal with the fallacious arguments we come across with. Should we confront them directly by simply naming the fallacy used? Should we put forward the logical form of the argument and argue why it is wrong?

Usually such direct methods would fail. Unless the person we are confronting is a logician and exactly knows what we are talking about, direct confrontation method could backfire. The one we are confronting could simply ignore such objection, and even if he or she is a logician, the conversation could easily become about the logic itself instead of the topic at hand.

However, what we usually can do is to use some obviously absurd example in the general form of the fallacy. Consider for example the fallacy of composition: "Everyone has a father and a mother. But it does not mean that say, a society also has a father and a mother." Or, in case of appeal to culture when we easily point out to a lot of things that people in a culture use to believe in, but were obviously absurd.

The matter could also be much clearer if we ask important questions. For example in case of appeal to culture we could ask "But, are you saying that whatever people choose is good?"

Furthermore, a part of human condition is our emotions. In many cases, human emotions motivate us in the short run much more than logic does, and these emotion (unfortunately or fortunately) attach themselves to our beliefs. We usually cannot expect our opponents to immediately abandon everything they believed simply because we name a fallacy.

We, you readers of this book and me as well, are also swayed by emotions. I don't think it's shameful to admit to making mistakes or be emotional, it is a part of being human. Being aware of this fact, knowing that we are also fallible, is by itself a great achievement in my mind.

And of course, we never have to forget to ask the theme question of progress, "Why?"

For further reading:

- "Crimes Against Logic" by Jamie Whyte,
- "Attacking Faulty Reasoning" by T. Edward Damer,
- "The Snake and the Fox: An Introduction to Logic" by Mary Haight,
- "How to Think about Strange Things: Critical Thinking for a New Age" by Theodore Schick and Lewis Vaughn,
- "Logic: A Very Short Introduction" by Graham Priest.
- "42 Fallacies" by Michael LaBossiere

Printed in Great Britain
by Amazon